HEARTBEAT ON LOVER'S STREET

HEARTBEAT ON LOVER'S STREET

ANTONI DAVISON

With thanks for the cover illustration to
A-Figure-in-Black ©2018 at www.deviantart.com

A stark, often dark yet defiantly beautiful depiction of love amidst mental illness. Vividly voracious with an empty cupboard, seeking respite amongst ghostly glow of each night feeling fading and contrite. Halo looking back amidst an attack of black. Portion-like madness in season, sweeping pain of red rains tyrannical treason. In pillow talk whilst birds did natter and squawk found an illuminating tower granting salvations power throughout darkest and foulest solitudes drowning seas. My baby blue, thank you graciously for all you did do when everything seemed so trite and untrue. Took a dare when no energy spare to proceed with only defiant deserve a reserve to look up to parting black cloud. Love's incantations read levities loud.

Contents

Birthday in The Void...1

Nocturnal Nightmares..3

Love's Urban Warfare...4

Soldier of Misfortune 5

Stones on Eyes, Darkest Skies......................................6

Timeshare of Ghost Town Spare...................................7

Spaceman...9

Lucky Penny..10

Worrisome Whirlwind..11

Butterfly Endeavour 12

Red Sheet of Prior Defeat..13

Low Dance, Another Trance..15

Lover's Street..16

Park 17

Overpass on Crimson Grass...18

Cinnamon...19

Storm...21

Reverie..22

Statue..23

Creativity Born of Chaos..24

Woodland View Rejoicing Anew....................................25

Charm..27

Sanctuary 28

Torchlight...29

Burrow...30

The Time Is Now...31

True...32

Night Racing, Halo Facing 33

Downcast Past Racing Fast...35

Tropical Heat..37

Nectar...38

Vicious Traditions..39

Love's Smile..40

Light in Eyes...41

Paste...43

Dancing Grey..44

Caffeine 45

Roses Thorn of New Dawn..46

Auctioneer..47

Catacomb of Empty Threads...48

Southpaw Digging for More...49

Friday 50

Saturday..51

Sunday 53

Paradise Flower..54

Drowning Pools, Shimmering Jewels..............................55

Birthday in The Void

Since the moment I was born,
under a darkened sky how I used to mourn,
for I once was dying with empty breath,
father time tormented with each movement of his silence,
every day, every dream a nightmare,
future seemed nothing more than a torturous scare,
traceries of taunts from invisible hands all I had,
rejuvenation of my spirit I once thought impossible.

Oxygen destroyed emotion, passion, once golden forsook,
as I lay upon empty bed with all he took; this was my plea:
A way to believe and no more ways to deceive,
for my Judas to be banished from out of my mind,
for the past to stop torturing me and to leave it behind,
a life without sadness,
mankind without madness,
memories without the fracturing sorrows,
highs without the cavernous hollows,
seven days to live life without strife,
serenity without chaos,
for a being to answer my plea,
for love to be allowed to be,
for God to walk the land,
for another set of footprints along my own in the sand.

The monumental pursuit of a dream I once believed to be
roads to fault,
but still I did not cease or halt,
the clouds above all appeared so grey,
in the silence, I used to whisper and say:
Is this world already forsaken?
Did my hope vanish or was it taken?
Why is my world so barren and stark?
Where is my light banishing the dark?
Who is there that really does care?
How long can I contain this solitude that I bare?

I know now that suffering is mandatory,
for the moments of chaos breed the most serene glory,
hope induces ability to cope through darkest story,
I beg myself to see inside eye of mind, leave past behind,
inside is written and signed with testimony of sorrow,
but another day is tomorrow, I'll shed this hellish hollow,
I will persevere when grim reaper of doubt is upon me,
for life is a maze, yet guides are all around,
though they may not make a sound.

Nocturnal Nightmares

Broken down, universal, first rehearsal of life, blade of
knife, strife to the wrist, paroxysms making a fist, dark
blemishes, shadows twist, losing my head, world spinning
on repeat with my ruinous defeat. Cannot remember for a
moment in which restaurant we met. Faith tied and bound,
mouth glued shut, cannot call out or make a sound,
no other is around, falling, flashes of the ground,
grey pavement today, early morning doom harsh bloom.
Who are those figures that loom? Lost without a clue,
thought I was getting gold, has solace been sold?

Afraid of the date I first died, my love, my love, they lied in
dead chambers. May pulsing streetlight, lost you last night,
once bright, strikes of midnight, seas of solitude swallowed
my soul, spitting out my bones, who owns my face? Grace
lost; at what cost? Shuddering silence; bitterest embrace.
Sister midnight wears my teeth; such dreams, coming apart
at seams. Generations denied a poltergeist host. I can still
outrun into the sun. Satellite burning bright lost your will.
Feelings sinisterly slide, cannot hide. Wings cannot glide.
Love does abstain all the pain inside heart and brain.

Love's Urban Warfare

Constellations sucking me dry, falling sky, oversaturation
curling my skin, such queen of liberty, losing power of
speech, losing the world's reach, where is the wisdom you
taught? Darkness such a lecherous leach. Sucking at my
genesis. Running through the gloom, such doom inside.
In our home, I slam door shut and hide, inside you are there
stood, wearing a hood and holding a torch, flickering battery,
all understood. Just a dream, love is still on my team,
tears gleam into embrace. Such a beautiful face.
Life feeling like a race, can I keep this purposeful pace?

Took me for a ride into there, where weaknesses laid bare,
we share stories of obtuse oblivion's dawn, you did mourn,
yet we saw new dawns fawn celebrating rational days stay.
Been floating here too long on this rock that does shock,
hands on clock, wounded rhymes, explosions in the sky,
why? Reconcile with style, hush, you say with finger to my
rampant mouth, every word slipping and spinning south.
There was loss and fear, always near, time froze, all of the
seasons cold and dark at once. Earth stopped spinning with
everything dimming. Sign above scrawled by love.

Soldier of Misfortune

World at your command, serenity banned,
didn't have the golden ticket in my pocket,
pulled out eyes from foresight's socket,
everything that rises going ghastly wrong,
belonging to dread head bed, empty song,
karaoke of an empty orchestra, furious
gathering storm inside did just deform
though love has no shape or abject form.

You came to me, wonderful weed killers,
poured on everything I once adored,
blooming blossoms from archaic ash,
my brother and sister that did crash,
so many plans we never ever lived,
though through your pragma I sieved,
darkness became so far reaching,
ardour now tremendously teaching.

Stones on Eyes, Darkest Skies

Paradigm shift of me, all now adrift
on River Styx, bound by my bricks,
this decadent disorder twisting tricks
into my mind, world left me to bliss blind,
getting away from this tomb of my room
where darkest shadows doom in the gloom.

Underneath floorboards of me abstractly
an impending cavernous catastrophe,
Viciousness; can't flick the switch inside,
lights help and discipline darkly denied,
cannot let go, wilted weeds on heart grow,
help me called with lunacy to skies above.

Thus; a collapse, dilapidating decay I say,
manically high, fell apart like voices said,
vexing voice ringing with sinister singing
echoes off cage walls, end to me calls,
silence suffering with penances pillow,
bury me underneath weeping willow.

Though a saviour's survival shout,
leave this punishing place, out, out, out,
into arms of nurturing nature of living,
glimmering shimmering pond, hero heron,
each beating of wings brings a calling
to recognise, fervour surrounds so arise.

Timeshare of Ghost Town Spare

Devilish blur knocking on door, yearning absolute for more,
midnight seeking desperately smell of sunshine to be mine.
Night is long, full of terror of devotion to poisonous potion,
I will not forget, this tonic beside under sheets is now set.

Done all I can, ravaging ruinous decay disorderly dancing,
everything a disaster, violent void advance furiously faster,
bleeding sky raining fallen birds to underworld's glooming,
booming collapse looming, another fickle fallen dooming.

O lord, deliver me from beggar's banquet of soil and dust.
Reality casting shadow, empty cupboard. Leave this place,
we must. Trust. Lost my reserve and faith without a trace.
Bank account empty as my hope, falling off financial slope.

Freezer bare, vines around heart viciously ensnare.
God break down this black door, surely there has to be
more than this everyday everything broken all at once, of
ash scattered face on cotton papers despairing disgrace.

Bliss burnt, curtains drawn, on this blackened day I truly
mourn, lost my resolutions learnt and freedoms earnt.
Yesterday's hymn to lost reflection, poverties plastic
smelted melted plate, infestation in mind to eradicate.

Mounds of mould from lies sold, they said it would get better, endlessly on records repeat, said you planet hopping jet setter. Found mound of a grass covered in crimson, endless dreams, destitute depraved demons pulling apart my frayed seams.

Nightmare, living in a ghost town, no living thing here at three AM, running whilst ghosts of past gunning, some nights forever with fragile sights, back against the wall, to the sky I clutch at clouds and to an underworld I fall.

Though now everything gleams far as I could see, saviour not way up high beyond red sky found me. Scooped ice cream to serve in a dish for me a wish, my nebula nurse, you lifted and sifted in this wreck an answer to tilt neck.

Breaking circles curse, looking up to parting black sky, raining ceasing red rain and pain, from way up high, I believe you fell to fix my wounded wings, morning sings with possibility bringing hope in creativity of all things.

Spaceman

Drowning frowning, mires misery,
fear this road I strode will liquify,
swallowing soul whole till I die,
submerging in regret then set
with me a spaceman statue
from when I ventured into
endless dark, alone lost
my spark, yet a lark
did glide beside
filling my hide
with bliss
a kiss.

Lucky Penny

In barren empty shop, closing time, time to mop,
came yelling tell, contrite clutches, I fell to sinister spell,
stumbling with empty stomach rumbling, reality crumbling,
my last rusted penny did drop beside bloodied mop,
down gaps in grate, I did morosely contemplate
stale bread on shelf with mould rife in my head.

All living things inside of me walking bleeding dead,
pleaded with the keeper whilst the world receded,
wilted rose on shelf knowing heartbreak takes,
needing water from entire world's supplicating lakes,
net strewn across stars, glancing light off cars,
you venture into night illuminating all bright.

Offering reason, breaking twisting pains treason,
mouth musing, your words amusing, going south,
catching sight of us in reflection; hidden and divine.
Perfect life, you offered me the breaking bread,
virus pale, my thanks so frail, starlit trail in skies,
pardoning, purifying with honesty, love's wisdom wise.

Worrisome Whirlwind

Bones of me a dinosaur under black tar,
affection digging and searching for more
beyond death's brittle broken black door
of dying constellations with sorrowful soot
underfoot, do tread carefully please,
dreams of me like egg shells beneath.

Feet fragile, dancing in thunderstorms,
greeted the veiled visiting witch in ditch
and forked road, white horse she strode,
skeletal prance allowing my advance,
second chance in helicopter whirling
through skies with suffering silence.

Charging vessel, own body in my arms
with spiritual bride sequined beside.
They say in heavenly hold so far above:
there are no husbands and wives,
be free from labels here, love strives
to certainty and serenity amidst our lives.

Butterfly Endeavour

Million miles away, lost to garish greys,
turning sand, man may be an island,
modern transport triumphs the journey,
ours just begun, race of a creed chase,
chasing of a butterfly when a boy coy,
unfurling wings, perching on the swings.

Though now a man sorrow now stings,
optimism; multi-coloured light in prism
on flag or displayed proudly on bag.
Humanity saw some good light
though when all fades to doors dark
we are all made from same soul spark.

So why segregate beyond grace's gate?
We all share at the end same one fate,
some harvest dreams from fellow teams,
stealing away a song to belong on here.
Mother Earth weeping as we're sleeping,
my own eternal darkness now creeping.

Red Sheet of Prior Defeat

Start has just begun,
sun shining to run,
race of a creed chase,
God help me my sun,
bloody eye in graces face,
they pray to stay,
dignify thus place.

Hey I'm waving
whilst the blue clouds
parting and saving.
Gratitude holy shrouds
whilst hades be paving.
I'm good thanks, home
with my plastic comb.

Saturday night spike,
green troubled trike,
memory of a grey day,
tractor's combine harvester,
wooden box afire,
blonde blue eyed her,
hearse punctured tire.

Saddest thing I've seen:
mobility scooter broken down
beside cemetery junction,
my smile departed solemnly,
frown of angel's solemn frown,
witch dancing with veiled gown,
hand punctures earth free.

Horse and carriage
coupling antiquity,
hold the raindrops,
sunshine glorious today,
hall's winter wonderland
pulled me out quagmire
with a turning egg timer.

Low Dance, Another Trance

Dreaming like a low dance another trance
of mitigating marriage upon railway carriage.
Can I earn this serendipitous second chance?
Waking harsh breaking, thinking of fleeing,
seeing startled deer dart past prance,
announcer on crackling mic, feeling pain
in taut chest like an intravenous spike,
cannot hear single word, sounds like
a convoluted ghost host and dreamlike.

Sweetness I've tasted such bitter fruit
rotten to core, do not sell me anymore.

Grinding wheel turns in September,
meeting holistic heaven's member,
this journey for you I do so adore,
yet I cannot escape macabre minds
loneliest spell, even my Jesus son fell.
Throughout May repeating it is today,
reliving horrific haunting hollow hell,
lost it all from horrid height so tall,
clouds rope, we can certainly cope.

Lover's Street

You are golden ground beneath my fragile feet,
gracefully guiding down illustrious lover's street,
saving grace with a smile beaming on my face,
anointing stranger, we meet with serene grace,
once beseeched by such a solemn frown,
I was haunted by a malicious monstrous maze.
Sinister serpents came on my mind to graze,
each step down a slab did disastrously stab,
putting all in a draconian deathly daze.

Steel cold on first date with my rising fate,
passing into cemetery junctions gate,
yet succulent food on my porcelain plate,
serene gift and shared suffering we sift.
With words of dread spilling out my head,
your smile, love's beaming sun rising above.
Love of baby blue calling my name aloud,
this defiant decree fixing melancholy me,
no longer wearing ripped burial shroud.

Park

On your wondrous wisdoms I have sipped
as into olive oil our brown bread dipped,
spreading wings once clairvoyantly clipped.
Parks dark life slithering and scuttling
though no fear is near in darkness here,
sirens alarm, you handed such a charm,
relief from the red condemning thief.

Overpass on Crimson Grass

Manic depressive, past repressive,
silent scream in alcove of chaotic cove,
transcripts blotted ink, black I again sink
into borderline barrages bustling brink,
think your way out of this opaque one,
fear rife, certainty nefariously gone,
adoration absolute, hostelling here.
Endlessly falling, your smile stalling
ruthless gravity from tired and the hurt,
moss covered grave sprinkled with dirt.

Hand punctures earth free, this is me
pulling punctuation's parcels apart,
cherished gifts from hosanna heart,
saviour smiles, sunlight stretches for miles.
Hard times, funeral bell so often chimes,
not for me today, granted reason to stay,
in just one night banishing years of fright,
lost to endless midnight, nothing bright
yet I rejoice in your tender visage's voice,
watering seeds not of sorrow tree creeds,
Philia; many forms quenching the storms.

Cinnamon

Cinnamon sweet spreading on morning toast,
crimson hair beauty shimmering serenely fair.
Adore what you feel a chore in self wealth a guide
for eyesight's trueness of vision not to again hide.
Silver of you my mystery, hands of you mine spare,
serendipitous story of elderly care freeing any compare.
Reach cans on top shelf, pass around supermarket aisles,
graces graceful face gratefully reinventing sunrise styles.
Stranger smiles soothingly. Offering thanks of course,
aren't you a most pretty one? Freeing elderly remorse.

Funny story from a far-away city now departed,
love's salvage and restitution blissfully started.
Calming waters dowsing furious fire my head,
crystal pouring light beside candles so bright.
Dearly gifting and lifting, sifting amongst dread
offerings once falling off planet to sea of dead.
Princess hands of my pure purposeful prince,
clandestine name, for now let's call you Vince.

Prior fantasy of life stuck in traffic lights,
always on redemption as wings truly bled.
Been searching depths of maps mind in head,
waiting to see my muse for a long way too much today.
Phantom ballet on repeat, defeated were my feet,
gliding through, no colours in me with people I meet.
I see a door once painted black tar on the inside,
universe is no more mystery; I will always be my lord's lord.
Got the music in me kissing my ear with all I that I adored
and you are plucking strings of my heart like a harpsicord.

Storm

A band of fallen brothers that times quicksand smothers,
tiny raft carrying my decree to finally see the light in me.
Satellite shining nurse from balcony on this midnight curse,
away from northern star forgetting route of my rusted car.
Time stamped departing yet my nurse this isn't a hearse.
Dark cosmic universe offering reply through fog tainted sky,
phone pings and heart sings, just trash talk turning to ash.

Checking every word text, obsessive compulsions flexed,
pouring another glass of wine awaiting sanctifying sign,
pardoning absent waiting, phone illuminates as though
conscripted by those golden gates. Message sent to repent
from my tears fallen on younger years, now you have leant
an indestructible umbrella, sheltering from corrosive rain
that flooded and corroded surviving synapses in my brain.

Every tap brings thoughts of the time you rap as I lay down,
each word eulogy to how you are fixing rotten apple in me,
into sleep we together weep and laugh at my moods chart.

Reverie

You are calming the tides of all harshest seas,
granting more breath than a thousand oak trees,
a gracious thank you for embracing love so true,
sorry for intrusive interlopers and silly things I do.
When apart counted down are days upon the chart,
together a great magnitude of colour in the heart,
black holes and revolutions unity again embraces,
illuminated are distant faces in forsaken places.
As the memory returned once ensnared in vines
blossoms and grows, overlapping tomb's signs.

Your love so gloriously shows torchlight in me,
answer previously locked and lost was the key.
My colours buried under house are now found,
once felt small like a worm in barren ground.
Shimmering contrasting symmetry of three,
glory to be in this trinity answering my plea.
Colossal thank you for self-sacrificial choice,
kindness of compassionate volunteered voice.
My mellifluous and marvellous musing violin
soothing my fragile and brittle broken skin.

Statue

Went on down to town again,
chain pulling like dungeon rein.

Enter bliss that we miss, so much to gain,
chaos remains inside masked soul stain.

Broken statues to all forsaken I did take,
demons slain did at once seem to wake.

Levee of the lake did surge and break,
tidal oncoming unreal and fickle fake.

Where scarred hearts burn and sear,
imprinting tear of wretched burning fear.

Quieten sad song, to love I belong, you hear?
Solitary imprint of another abstract alien tear.

Creativity Born of Chaos

Haunted by memory of a place inside a better me
with dignity and sovereignty erstwhile company.
Angels' promises dart, when apart hopes flee,
lighthouse interjects, saving from deathly sea.

Seeing in store reflection a ghastly ghost
as arresting sorrow became my host.
Away from my passion I love the most,
longing to be with you on sunlit coast.

Mr hangman advances with the rope,
this grey today saying I cannot cope.
Insidious notions advancing interlope,
defiantly, erroneous end I say nope.

Woodland View Rejoicing Anew

Late night yearning fuelling fires burning
whilst sheltered sinuous heads turning.
Tip tap tapestry a freedom of me,
net in the sea only caught debris,
nocturnal animals scurry from burrows,
we eat our takeaway curry in a hurry,
plastic knife and fork in the road.

Sat on ground quietly in no sound,
dust plumes across sky and bat flies by,
helicopter searching spotlight from high,
passing into a field with succulent yield,
horse cart apart from languishing leader,
story read by torchlight, resplendent reader.

Allegories voice magnificently musing,
in my mind it was always midnight,
ephemeral light so evanescently bright,
day glow fades to below melted snow
from tainted tears of penances show.

In the stars above your name signed,
leave perpetual vortexes past behind,
struggling through to me and you,
what can we together daringly do?

Defiantly got life mutually for you,
baby it is forever and always true,
my shimmering aquamarine hue.

Blessed be in the celestial crew,
truly faiths tested invested a clue
pristinely calming everything anew.

Charm

Your name becomes my celestial charm freeing from harm,
cherished locket pulled from God's gracious giving pocket.
Everyday sun did arise, I was in trouble with love's rubble,
saw you turn water to wine, every possibility now double.

Sanctuary

Drowning my doubts in a reaffirming city
harmonising me with such true serenity
with a captivating perpetual delight.
Coalition of senses a freedom page,
I'll take you soon to my stage,
prior chains did brittle and enrage.
Inspiring muse; past is old news,
beautifully witty, so divinely pretty.

Torchlight

Fear is all I did know,
never one to show
my true lord is my light
shining so brilliantly bright,
scorching away fright
of a forbidden sight
so majestically true.

Lifted from an abyss
with most gratifying kiss,
such captivating bliss
unifying trinity of me,
such majesty in unity.

No more to decay
in splintered worlds we say
live life free within me,
my favourite stay,
living in today.

Burrow

Once full of broken thought I could not repair,
could not venture outside from languishing lair,
lost ability to hope for frayed searching rope.
Dead man in my bed he said, looking back,
men in black, bleeding from life's attack,
it's a different life today, rise from this away.
Don't cry, arise from the forsaking floor,
there has to be more than this black door,
it will be alright; thousand candles bright.

Veiled faces praying for my staying,
wash away soul's stains, take it slow,
hand-wash, rinse and repeat, dangle from feet,
hang me up to dry on spiritual clothesline,
bring a ladder when the brightness returns.
Lately found such a racing rejoicing sign,
consciousness and reality again burns,
lost myself without a trace in this place.

Ghouls did invade cracks and enter
into heavy backpacks pulling me down,
sorrowful pain, crimson chief down insane,
sinner found saints that beautifully paint
stars into the gloom once endless doom.
Sun will always arise from deepest cloud,
life is a treasured graceful gift so be proud.
My darling so far yet so close from reach
so many words of wisdom forty did teach.

The Time Is Now

For it is the very nature within us all,
to love
then destroy,
then to love again
knowing only pain,
this is the searing fire of fear
banish it from whence it came.
Love is no game,
love conquers fear,
fear torments,
love soothes.
Do not fear love,
do not knowingly destroy love,
only to love again when it is too late,
pleading another chance from white gate.
See in the dark my sanctifying spark,
you are my deal to when all is stark,
guiding my angelic lights highway.
Love blossoms on our entire stay,
live free in beauty today.

True

Love can be such a tragedy,
where the constant longing becomes torture,
where we sell our souls,
where compromise ruins our lives,
where we forsake ourselves.

This you see,
is not what love should be.

Night Racing, Halo Facing

Deepest darkest night perils causing midnight fright,
second sight found in your blue eyes such tranquil delight.
Fallen into you holding a magnificent sacrosanct rose,
colours wash from attack of confessional black prose.

Pacing, sleepwalking around the room, travelling light,
running late for a meeting with dreams beautifully bright,
wearing a backpack, slippers and scarf, stars in my eyes,
carrying a plastic beaker like the Holy Grail's eternal prize.

Snow I did shout, forgetting another is about, outside
into winter's frost; what does this expedition cost? I boldly
hold, imitation money from Mayfair sold. Behold I call
to the moon, holding a pizza cutter like a sacred rune.

Stay away shouted to fabled monsters. Clutching metal box
a shield and banner I yield with emblem of curious red fox,
sword plastic, fantastic I screamed. Unholy creatures fell,
tapping on shoulder. You wear a hooded sweatshirt.

What are you doing stood in your best slippers in dirt?
You laugh loud as I hold chicken dippers like grenades.
You going to bury those in our garden with a spade?
Look, you say, at all the holes you have already made.

Looking deeply into your oceanic flooded blue eyes,
noticing you wear with a tear, warrior's warlike disguise,
shield of dustbin lid you hold and clothes pole you stole
from the land underneath my walking waking dreams.

We command our invisible factions and all the teams,
windows of neighbourhood watch twitching curtains,
as we battle the dark-side of cruelty with a hair brush,
fighting frivolously giving such a graceful freeing rush.

Throughout the entire morning, others nearby snoring,
we vanquish deliveries of destitute with magic flute,
this is when I did know, our fondness will always grow
throughout any horrors hour or darkest crumbling tower.

Kissing over victory, pulsing through celebrating crowd,
tender honey glowing with warmth of you always knowing,
baby, you are miracles warmth of serendipities showing,
with you my cup of nectar is everlasting and fully flowing.

Downcast Past Racing Fast

Beast dreams in total darkness
stealing the everything of me,
blotting expectations from journey.
Poles north and south
spilling from my morose mouth,
sun outside thawing ice on heart
advancing another flood,
anything you want, you know I would
though today is like giving all my blood.

Everything in reverse,
a broken verse.
Why can I not stop thinking of you?
Breathe you in.
Breathe you out.
Voices inside howl and shout
from traces of your soft skin.
Together for purities night we were true.
Morning became a curse,
everything in reverse.

Chasing my dreams,
as they run away
I fade to grey.
Second chance
come dance with me.

Teach me your song
to belong with solidarity.
Winter's memory a dead cold
to have and to hold.
Another fading photograph,
counted days like a graph.
You flickered like beautiful gold,
melted thoughts I cannot mould.
Falling through a void to avoid.

Looking to pools on polluted ground,
hellish hands creeping out,
banishing them, enchanting sound
on my name daringly devout,
singing to me my muse
beyond a simple passage
round a ruined roundabout,
sacredly you are evicting my doubt.

Tropical Heat

Such fragile beauty in all he seeks,
different universe found me a nurse
to relieve pain of black blood flowing
down drain, feeling disorderly insane,
such laughter on repeat with knowing,
wondrous wings, affirmative aeroplane
fly us away to where I am again sane,
to the tropical heat, sandals on feet,
lay my life's baggage handler down,
free me from this solemn frown,
arrest this thief in my town
that steals my smile,
wait just a while.

Nectar

Wonderful, wonderful filling my chalice until full,
lights bright bridge pulling from ridge in my skull,
creativity born of chaos lifting from abstract abyss
Reflection I didn't recognise, me I solemnly miss;
now paradise purifies in just one cathartic kiss.
Banner man waving our fervent freedom flag,
diamante glimmering skull on black tote bag,
a ghost made real with transcendence I feel,
bunting made with harmony a parade of teal,
this love is my cure for endless black door,
dancing on sequined sails seeking more.
I never did believe in love at first sight
until its candle illuminated all bright,
hands of hope outstretched before,
love's smile, graciously my cure.

Vicious Traditions

Contradictive words I now do sieve,
searching for a nugget amidst dirt,
vanquishing all my hurt with you,
guides map doused in the tap,
banishing the grey country,
beyond this world's sight,
pious and contrite,
falling into night.

Love's Smile

For if love were to have a face
it would be the one with the most grace.
If love were personified it would forever dance,
love would be the one where there is a second chance.
Its smile would be as radiant as the sun,
it would tell me that my journey has just begun,
dancing cosmic chaos yet always fun.

Light in Eyes

Torchlight permeates darkness of another perpetual midnight, captain of this plane landed on water carrying all he taught her. In his backpack a book of wisdom and vision of investment intentions, useful affirmations change his name to holy incantations from tensions. On deserted island: skull and crossbones point the way to leach of today; sucking on my faith in love because no sign of surreptitious dove. He is waiting at gates across land of overwhelming fickle fates, kept company in this unholy land by dates marked on love's chart. Rag and bone man scuttles by with wooden leg and clothes peg, hanging his garments by the fire, ashes smoke on which we choke. He utters three words: the lasting confession, an unusual transgression.

Tells a story of surviving a landing gory amidst sandstorms fury, with his blissful bride by his side and packets of nut underfoot. Landed on this unfortunate abode yet they sauntered and strode into unknown with only one glory to each other magnificently shown; their admiration. Kissing of lands gone by yet they did not solemnly sigh. For they had their own hands to hold and kept company with stories told. Necklace of rope and shell, all other material gifts from memory fell. This land once thought hell, a gratifying tropical story to our children tell. In kindred kingdom; their endearment made a boat keeping them afloat. Catching in net, setting free all regret. Simple dish set on quaint plates made of wood yet only one greeted. Expectation fleeted.

The man finds courage through falling tears that his wife did perish yet keeps him company on this day, everything he cherished. Seeing you in this story, beautiful faltering parade we once made. As the man digs on the beach with a tiny bucket and spade; he teaches everything their love made without interceptors to invade, his will and testament made a doll out of reeds and offers this. Everyday offer a kiss to those one day we may morosely miss because in spiritual land a reunion is met from every prior bliss, with lights in their will and an unlimited amount of skill beyond pill. Let calming waters of our love douse fire and be our cup to fill. My avenger loves defender did say, hold singular grain of sand in hand; all is mighty within this great land.

Paste

They say a love like ours will not last
as the skies above us grey to overcast.
Locked inside a horrific horror of past,
countless losing relief to mournful thief.
Bound to a black book with all they took,
world's earthquake again to us shook.
Searching your face for that fixing look,
paper moulded you out of paste.
Yet our love not near filled with fear,
tossed me today to the acrylic waste.

Dancing Grey

Compromise just complicates as love waits,
waits for no mankind, leave this ghost behind.
In the apostle action useful meeting fleeting,
found me an absolute gem of a find.
Imperfections glimmer through
to me and you, what can we do?
Find our way out of this breaking one,
Earth runaway cast me out of today.

Caffeine

Clouded thoughts of dismay lingeringly stay unjustly
uninvited, staring to skies with wounded cries demanding
you be knighted. For you have slain many a demon from
wild wilderness of my brain, where paths were blocked with
all this world shocked so insane. Retreat, retreat, perils
together we defeat and unison's wisdom meet. Friends
message, love sends such a loving expression we greet.
Retaliation of my depression a wraith-like sinister shadow
appearing. Reverie and rejoice, in my eye I am fearing as
greener grass nearing. Surrounding a cascading stream
with tiny pebbles radiant under sun, joys to my heart on
this journey through true nature's blessedness begun.
Bridge across a great ravine so steep the end for us cannot
be seen, stumbling to rat nest, scurry in a hurry as though
overdosed on caffeine. Can't shake this little feeling foe
will continuously grow and grow, yet this is our battle and
we will not fall like cattle with deplorable death's show.

Roses Thorn of New Dawn

Love and desire should know no boundaries, sweeter than entire world's confectioneries. As tonight whispers in my ear banished is fear and instead belief realised, this is going to be a great year. Quieter we become more awake to revelations we may not hear, shed no remorseful tear my well spirited dear. Progressing to harmonious opportunity free with such luxurious beauty. No longer free falling through ruthless gravity. One with pure serenity. Wondrous wonderland placating plastic fake demand of treading in sinking sand. Spiritual toll booth I did once pay. Know our heart is true when within a clear view where everything been through is just means to write a majestic message of today where it is only sonorous hope hereditary I convey.

Auctioneer

Auctioneer holding my conviction, selling more jewels
of crystallised tears from late years, they fell like pools.
My once estimated value a dreaded detached zero
though rubies, diamonds and pearls I do not own
treasured are those that save, this world's true hero,
love's treasure chest bequest thawed a glacier heart
and flooded what was once proficient in dancing flame,
eternal engineer thanks for second gear and new start.

Catacomb of Empty Threads

Skeletons on black and white wall standing so tall
as my icy tears again fall to karaoke of ghostly ball,
stars plucked from night sky as one of us wears a tie,
trembling hands, our progress they attempt to deny,
dug a ditch becoming a cavernous rippling ravine
yet you hold my hands still, such a glorious queen.

Southpaw Digging for More

Walking in pardoning park sunlight fading to disparaging dark, feelings so stark. Holding hands with air because you are not there alongside trees' wilted branches. Black dog following me, unseen by a stranger life so serene as he will emptily bark. Depletive desolate depths seen with nirvana been. On readying resolute ranches, this loyal animal caged inside so long; nowhere in this paradise does it belong. Unfed gnarly beast deserving great feast yet single can afforded by hollow man, serenity and justifying solace I seek yet this black coated sentry with me so long.

Growling as people near, scaring away pairing of whole weeks can, ringtone tossed ahead a nutritious bone for me to own some reaffirming respite. Each syllable you speak guiding onto celestial creek with sanctifying sandy shore. Curtains close on this day with scars in stuttering words I say emptily to night. Laying down the bone as a toll to the spirits seeking trophy of penances pure paw. Bounding into the oceans; trumpets and choirs clap with a frisbee thrown, anointing waters from god's weeping daughters for mutt that playfully rolls as through nirvana our love strolls.

Friday

As I carefully choose my shirt I notice a speck of dirt
not on my shirt; one injustice born of horrendous hurt.
So many images of you dressed so opulently scatter,
withering spectral harlequins boisterously natter,
their voice looming, world falls with their consuming,
they seek an offering dusting my lips of assuming,
memories encased in frame carrying piteous blame,
pardon drips of blood in pools of sinuous shame.

Saturday

With shattered glass into their kingdom I pass,
no buildings grown, such disorder once grass,
kingdom of ash from distant crash a sorrow tree,
realm a construct of anguishing absolute anarchy,
resolute tomb of weeping bride of endless doom,
pursuing whirling winds, nothing here in bloom.

Yet I display a photo of you and she smiles,
inflicts on me moment I rained tears on tiles,
though one word beckons all she reckons,
conjured a knife of strife in mere seconds,
love, let it be love, let it be love from above,
summoning a bird of paradise and a dove.

I say on bended knee my love here endlessly,
seen across the ghostly ghastly sickening sea,
everyday uninvited this mortal coil did smother
my prided protective cautionary spiritual brother,
mankind will prevail and we together will not fail,
no sustenance as this wraith's bread is all stale.

Sensing despair of silence brings microcosm tear,
I bring a glimmering guardian light where all is fair,
in this storm of eternity an undying endless midnight
she shares her fright where once stood a delight,
one departed, another kingdom born, she is torn
between darkness and bright; dying stars are worn.

For her lover did evolve and seek problem to solve,
testing resolute and archetypal atrocities resolve,
two become one when the other eternal gone,
in nothingness remained this remainder one,
patiently waiting grace of his most celestial face
though nothing came but rain on barren place.

Injustice did echo as quietly she began to let go,
though from tear a beautiful tree here does grow,
love the saviour and answer spreading a spark,
evolution from continuous cosmic dreaded dark,
creatures created an offering to erstwhile lover,
booming voice resolute in choice breaks cover.

Sunshine glorious, this bountiful beginning begun,
race of a creed chase, glorious glint, waters run,
fountains flourish, love again here does nourish,
bathing in waters free from ages cage we flourish,
free from bells ringing death of constructed time,
thunderclap of skies, angelic choirs again chime.

Hardship of dismay and decay dips, taking sips,
pure waters, again she smiles, holding on with grips,
sorrow tree falls, flying in sauntering shawl of fish,
we together laugh with succulent fruit in mosaic dish,
turning to me she says: I'm a believer, god's receiver,
love is the answer and greatest of the cosmic weaver.

Sunday

Day of rest coupled with the best
separated from reticent remorseful rest,
shared solidarities soliloquies of me
with the interminable infinite I confessed,
saint got tasking of writing down my asking
for loving lullabies to rain from the skies.

Ceremony of investing innocence,
tired and the hurt as we fell down to dirt,
dark storm affiances another alliance,
I'm going through the wild darkness
with eyes wide open yet you see through
to saintly sanctification white doors.

Falling rain and purple light purifying,
sorrow tree once me where arms branches,
legs once consumed by a fickle dying earth,
the last departing because freedom starting,
everything now endlessly to this love tries,
we reconcile poles piled recycling of X-ray.

Paradise Flower

My many ally, glimmering progress I will not deny,
as you light the candle on black flowers bedside,
whispering whirling smoke, into my arms you slide,
falling asleep in my encompassing evangelical embrace,
chandelier reflecting such celestial celebration's face,
through eternal white arches love magnificently marches,
lovingly restoring punishing past paroxysms as your snoring,
this love my resurrecting messiah and will never ever tire.

Reconciling relief, thank you, wondrous worlds depend,
gracious gratitude for constructing a more positive attitude,
with your valued visits, cards and well wishes you did lend,
for all those times, a sheltering arm and flowers they send,
freeing curse from violent visitations vexing vortexes verse,
stared into void, so much I have since euphorically enjoyed,
broke free from locks surrounding me, that once dragged,
you all clipped away vines on my heart that once snagged

Drowning Pools, Shimmering Jewels

In vacant places thoughts build to regretful races,
lost life haunts lingeringly, smell of you in traces
on the pillow and in silent words in fragranced air
whispering now where wisdom once fervently fair;
woodland nurse fixed tear in dark cosmic universe
though now to eternities garden where you reside
I can only offer you another black broken verse.
Tranquillity descended amongst all dying leaves
when off this planet you rose, my soul stuck here
with fear and dread running circles through head
and isolation ignited only returning burning year
as the yellow flowers turned again blotted brown
I became alone a dead man walking in this town
staring and despairing we may not meet again.

Cemetery junction contrasting to Lover's Street;
through the fog of another realm I see you there
looking back, hand and hand with seraphim hold
knowing your effect and impact on this land bold.
Bolder than the entire collective that haunted me
and attempted to wash me away to solitude's sea;
you expel perceived insanity making me feel free.
Turning to me in ruinous realm of stifling slumber
with insidious insomnia; my only company tonight
wishing I could sleep for a beautifully better number
and gain some deserved rectifying reigniting respite.
Face of remembered true grace here in this place
that exonerated all the planetary projected pain;
your hands reaching out and aspiration awakens.

I scrawl a story indiscernible to the naked eye
of when you smiled dipping to eggs so runny
by a woodland stove, silence absurdly funny.
Lasting messages that love can no longer die
gave me a reason to persevere and again try
with angel's tears raining down from sky
for those dearly departed that started here.
Though understanding where this ghost is standing,
my hope hit the ground with a breaking sound
yet a beautiful parade you all made for me
is the true conviction and testament of love;
truly from above this empty broken discord
you represent in personification death is cured.
Life is once again daringly and defiantly adored.